Isle of Joy

Other books by A.M. Caratheodory
    Amphibian Dreams
    Fragments (of Leukippus)
    Light from a Vanished Forest
    Wild Apples
    Forgotten Ruins
    Guarded by Trees

Other books at Mozart & Reason Wolfe Ltd
    The Thesis
    Two Diaries
    Tropomorphoses
    Cheap Visions
    Microscopia
    Lucifer Resplendent
    Musings
    Murmur
    Night Wolves
    Coyote Redux
    Waiting for Better Times (in Bulgaria)
    Redesigning the Planet
    RE: Viewing Turning Thinking
    Good Forestry
    Global Government
    Poetic Archaeology of the Flesh
    One Earth, Many Worlds (Holocosmology)
    Healing Animals & the Vision of One Health
    Ecoforestry
    Clearcut
    Domiture: Coevolution of Nature & Culture (OP)
    Radical Ecological Thought Experiments
    Basic Common Sense (More Experiments)
    Arcologies for the Planet (Coming Soon)

Isle of Joy

New & Selected Poetry
1966-2016

By A. M. Caratheodory

Art Work by Verona ReBow

Calliope Press
Mozart & Reason Wolfe Ltd.
Sarasota 2016

Copyright © 2016 by A. M. Caratheodory & Verona ReBow
All rights reserved under International and Pan-American
Copyright Conventions. No part of this book may be used or
reproduced in any manner without written permission from
the Publisher, except in the case of brief quotations embodied
in articles or reviews. All images and artwork is this book are
Verona ReBow's proprietary copyrighted works and may not be
reproduced without her permission. If you wish to license her art,
please go to http://www.veronarebow.com/pages/contact.html

Library of Congress Cataloging-in-Publication data
A. M. Caratheodory, 1946—
   Isle of Joy/A. M. Caratheodory

I. Title.
PS3553.A654A878 2016
ISBN-13: 978-0-911385-70-0
ISBN-10: 0-911385-70-3

A Calliope Press Book
Mozart and Reason Wolfe, Ltd. Wilmington, Delaware
Contact: Mozart@ReasonWolf.com

Design: Design@RianGarciaCalusa.com
Author: amc@3Muses.us

Manufactured in the United States of America
First Printing

1 2 3 4 5 6 7 8 9 10

Contents

Part 1. Overture
    The Others (of Plato)   9
    Authentic Fragments of Leukippus   12
    Another Song For The Road   13
    Wild Strawberries   14
    Drifting Away   15
    If You Could Live Another Hour   16
    Ode to Gaea   18

Part 2. Observing
    Mountain Light Trilogy   20
        (*Mountain Light / Age of Light / Metaphysics of Light*)
    The Ecstasy of Weeds / of Trees   21
    Cloud   23
    House Of Rain   24
    Driver   25
    Finger Play (STEM)   26
    Dancing between Shadows   29
    She Is One   31
    Deep Kiss   32
    Simple Time Travel   33
    The Future Unfolds With Us Inside   34
    Moonlight Lake   36

Part 3. Dreaming
    Wild Apples   37
    Bad Dream Coyote   41
    Eve In Dreams   42
    Lilith from the City   43
    Piñata of Dreams   44
    Ecology of Fire   44
    Floating Clearly   45
    Heart of Beauty   46
    The Reach of Water   48
    The Ground   49
    Leaves Fall and Turn   50
    Wolf Trilogy   51
        (*Wolf Loves to Hide / Wolf Story / Wolf News*)
    Shadow Play   53
    Changing Lightly with the Mountain   54

Part 4. Memories
    Mountain Bluebird Echo   55
    The Wasp   56
    My Heart Breaks   57
    Forgetting You   59
    Like Beasts   60
    Tain's Gift   61
    October Afternoon   64
    Perception Like Candlelight   65
    A Pharaoh's Sleep   65
    A Lady's Dance Card   67
    Druidess Of The Tuatha De Danann   68
    Picture Wall   70

Part 5. Imagining
    Amaryllis Falling   72
    Bastet Holding   73
    Heraklitus' Vision   74
    Aekus Humbled   75
    Bear Masks   75
    The Cave Of Night   76
    Alone In A World Of Wounds   77
    Convolutions (Whale Stories)   78
    Forest Passage   79
    Heartless   81
    Reflections on Surfaces   82

Part 6. Practicing
    Moments   83
    Aurum Nostrum   83
    De Origine Fabula   84
    Ille Terrarum   84
    Failing Sleep   85
    The Place Of Reconciliation   86
    Leaving Palouse   87
    Why You're Bad For Me   89
    Freedom & Practice   90

Part 7. Marishimira [In Bulgaria]
    Blue Stars   91
    Through Tearlight   92
    Our Daughter's Eyes   92
    In Wild Flight   93
    On Silk Pillows   94
    Snake Dance Flame Dance   95
    Gathering Layers: Cut Geode   97
    Propinquity   98
    Every Thread Made Visible   100
    Traces of Light   101
    One Little Drop   103

Part 8. Participating
    Three Perspectives From An Ancient Forest   104
        (*June, July, September, October*)
    Horses Under Lightning   107
    Light Pieces   110
    Swimming At Night in the Black Sea   111
    The Center Can Never be Reached   112
    Do Not Ask Me Why   113
    Is it Just a Smile?   115
    The Way of the Deer   116
    In a Vanished Forest   117
    Isle Of Joy   121

List of Art Works   123
About the Author   124
About the Artist   124
Colophon   125

Dedication by AMC

To Precious, first, the Marishimira of note.

To the Gang of Seven.

To Margaret, Mark & Emerson.

And to those who shaped my ideas, but who are not to be held responsible for how I expressed them: DLB, CJH, MLC, LJH, CLD, MWF, AN, GH, JBC, JGM, NL, LGMS, TB, VZB, NK, MB, TJ, and MN—as well as to Legend, Yang, Toma, Rebel, Chieftan, Mercedes, Grey, Athena, Crow-Magnon, Pan, Lad, Abelard, Heloise, Mina, Fric, Frac, Brigid, Oscar, Racer, Mina, Carbon, Hank-Ra, Willo, and the many more unnamed wild animal souls.

Dedication by VR

To my Parents, Family and friends who supported my vision and ambition:
Rolf , Hilde , Arlette, Jürgen, Allen, John, Yolanda, Sybille, as well to all the people animal Arthur, Sunny, Elvis, Angel, Jake, Betty, Phoenix , Java, Timor, Silver, Indi, and Kandiski.

And all the people animals who changed me for ever in the deepest way ...

Overture

The Others

"When he recalled his first home and the wisdom there,
And his fellow prisoners in that time, don't you suppose
He would consider himself happy for the change and pity
The others?"   Plato, *Republic* VII 516e

The world is washed with light; sky and rock
Are bleached white. There is the sea
And the faded green of trees.

To be as you taught, we thought we advanced
Toward perfection, but we became weary and lost—
Our tongues dried out. We perceived nothing
But intervals of light. We could not reach
Your ideal. . . . [nor] erase our origins.
You called us strange prisoners bound by our legs
And necks before shadows cast on the side
Of the cave by fires. You thought you freed
Us and dragged us up a rough, steep path.
You forced us to see the sun, source of the seasons
And steward of all things in the visible world.
From there we were led to contemplation of
What is best in the things that truly are.

But when we recalled our first home,
We longed for a world without weather,
Away from relentless, sun-driven change.
We longed to escape the weight of truth—
And then we found the cave again.
Let the hills take that unbearable mass
From our shoulders. Let the damp restore
Moisture to our skins and the dark
Return our dreams.

The abyss opened under our feet.
All we wanted from you, Platon, had not

The power to raise us higher—the dialectic
Does not lead upward, or outward;
There is no up or down, in or out,
Only the continuing spiral onward.

Where is the architect of the cave,
Whom we once praised? Welcome us back
With new designs. Make walls to keep
The sun from our eyes. We will use shadows
And mirrors to freeze its awful visage.

This is the place of life—the caves
Are not vacant, as the plains above.
We have made the earth secure with our
Own dark geography, comfortably bound.
This is our fathers' hearth. Savor
The aroma of cooking lamb—the senses
Expand—hear the trickle of water seeking
Its level through chiaroscuro rooms. Feel …

The caves are home. In filtered light
We polish the walls lustrous …
Ordained in the wombs of our mothers
To sow doubt in the entrails of the earth
We meditate in the depths and sleep
In the [narcotic] knowledge of rock. Mysteries
Leak into dreams inverted in negative infinity.

We press the limits of darkness down
To the limits of our illusions, insert
Ourselves in crevices of being—[matter's]
Center and the heart's, invisible.
We burrow in the [solidity] of rock
And build temples to feeling.

You taught us that the activity of art
Had the power to release us,
But art has its roots in darkness
And though its surface is displayed
For all, it seeks to intertwine things
With invisibility that we may see them.

We must play with shadows and live between
Perfect light and darkness, a double life.
This is the true song of the dialectic
Weaving voices into silence and twining
All things opposite around an empty center.

The sun impales forms; their colors
Are burned off. Light decomposes flesh
And only proud skeletons remain.

Wisdom is a wild thing like the Arcadian doe
And not easily captured with words. The dappled
Form leaves its shadow in our grasp while it slips
Away undaunted. A hunger we do not understand
Keeps us on the scent. We cannot give up the chase—
Nor can we ever catch her. [So] to be wise,
We must act as if the shadow is the doe.

Authentic Fragments of Leukippus (For FS 1974)

7.3   Images—violet-like—show us true being

8.2   The universe is held together by memory
 but everything is renewed by forgetting

8.8   ... [my] head is like a thundercloud where ideas flash
 and disappear leaving only bare tracks for memory.

11.2 To jump into a volcano is not the act of a god ...
 but to return is ... [and] who has seen
 Empedokles lately?

13.2.2   Who should I worship?
 Zeus and power? Aphrodite and love?
 ... the wind ... [I] choose Chronos
 —for time holds all power and love

13.4 The gods evaporate like clouds
 they came from nothing and left nothing
 behind, not thrones texts ruins or treasures—
 what man now petitions their return?
 if we exist in the image of our creators
 then we too must be nothing but clouds

21.1 We lose ourselves in images ... burn our [brains]
 with their brightness emitting blasts of sparks
 that fade ... the best turn to cinders in days.

22.3 ... flame is the flesh in bloom

26.7 In music the [stuff] of life is amplified beyond reason

27.0 ... ecstasy is a heart in which the sun distends

31.1 One records the most profound meanings
 the most ecstatic visions clumsily ... sporadically
 in fragments

Another Song for the Road (for DL 1966)

I laid down a road to her
Through the snow and ice
I walked it every evening
To bask in her new warmth
Her open acceptance and promise
Of things she, and I, did not understand.

Everywhere I went I made a road
And learned the landscape by heart
But when we married I strayed;
I was not sure what the goal was
And never tried to make a map.
I heard a song and knew it was
Like that somehow—I tried to move
To it, but it was too short and I lost
Sight of the meaning of togetherness—
Not to get somewhere or accumulate trash
But to hold each other close and dance
Watch the other, getting the steps to match.

And I learned, like lives and patterns,
Relationships are mortal, too,
And almost as delicate as the soul
Or the wing of a dragonfly.
I didn't know that then, when
I made so many unnecessary roads.

Wild Strawberries (for TB 1998)

On the way to fix the fence I walked over
them, but you called me back—hundreds
of tiny, ripe, wild, red strawberries,
almost invisible between bunches of grass.
We lay down next to a promising patch
and fed each other the sweet berries,
hardly aware that the horses had gathered
in the corner, looking to see if we
would share with them (we did).
We were slow, but they were patient.

I suppose we fixed the fence eventually
and rode the horses up the road, to see
the forest stream and stand in the shade
but of all the good times that we planned
and made, I remember this accidental
moment and smile—I swear that I can
still taste the juice that graced our lips.

Drifting Away (for LGS 2013)

Here is how I lived my life:
I drifted somewhere and sometimes back.
I never stopped until I drifted into a trap—
Caught in a trap! Something that denied my
Drifting so I broke it. Violence works sometimes.
Not always physical, it can be spitting out
angry words or slipping emotional bonds.
My love of drifting, of moving, of random sights,
Was greater than the comfort of being held.
I never thought I might change when I was old.
My desire to see other 'wheres' could not be denied
And if other 'whens' were possible, I would have tried
To reach them, too, for a brief trial.

I only needed a hundred dollars to start
The next vital, accidental adventure.
It was so easy—drifting made my decisions,
Shaped my goals—and I became a quantum hero
Determined by others' decisions and interference,
Bumped by incidental forces into random motion.
It was the drifting I loved, the movement I sought
The sense of being carried by the universe so far,
Without intent or plans to study the flow,
Without being bothered to try to be successful,
Without being tortured by questions or meaning.
And, whenever I was trapped I fought
To be free again, for a while.

I wonder now if drifting is not a different kind
Of trap. But, it is oh too late, the die have rolled
and this time might be better—

If You Could Live Another Hour
(Just to Say Hi)

You would not have any hair
left, but we could laugh
about the power of our genes
or rather, our mother's.
We could laugh again
at the awkwardness
of being reborn just
to see each other now
with sudden joy—touch
each other, both knowing
that you had no experience
after that moment of panic—
like rushing at a closing door
because you did not know
its patterns or its timing
but you had to go then
to be outside the realm
of disappointment and pain
not realizing that you caused
more than if you had just cried
at not being kissed or loved
and threw that pain away
like a tattered baseball.
No, nothing else could soothe
your awful tension then—
I noticed you smooth
your sleeve under the coat
when that picture was taken.
I look intently in your eyes
Now, trying to get past
the liquid bronze to see if
I could read your thoughts—
but I could not,
they were hidden

And now you are just
a photograph that wraps
me in its motionless capture
with a few photons on paper.
I can brush my finger across it
and think to send some message
or—what? I don't know.
I cannot say, I just miss you.
I can barely sigh.

So now I softly pray
that you have gone away
to coral dreams in the ocean
of air under the darkness
between stars
where eidolons stay
invisible with the ecstasy
of hiding.

Ode to Gaea

Necklace of light on a blue pearl,
Bearer of life as well as light
Against a curtain of point-blank stars
As if the stage was too distant
To measure in cubits or parsecs.
How can we ever reconcile
The glowing bacteria in waves
Or a fungus mound on a forest floor
With the all encompassing dark
That barely nourishes the cast
Of points too far apart to see,
To communicate. Even the waves
Of our media tire and disperse
Before reaching the nearest
Planet. And our friends our lives
Are too closely focused
On our minuscule feats
To look up and see in awe
Or fear that we have no meaning
Beyond what little impinges
On our sphere, as it is spanned
In groups and decades—yet, we pray
That our thought is amplified,
So it may enrich the value
Of simple size, distance, dust
And we pray for a measurer
To joy in diversity as we joy
In the quantal acts possible for us
Unless we contribute only to chaos
And our planet, rather than as song,
Will be described as wreckage—
Ours, dragging other complex life,
Then the light, the pearl, the earth
Will blink out unnoticed.
We were the nemesis, the agent

Of death, not birth, not for long
And our sorry adolescence ends
By demolishing the threads
And cycles and communities.
Finally, we pray for the rats
And bacteria to survive and progress
Where we cannot, or would not.
But, for a while, it was possible,
For the order to expand. But,
Acts were not enough, nor drift
Nor goals or ideas or hopes.
They were only scattered in bits
Before extinction met us early.
It was not fate, but our own fault.

I wish that I knew nothing
Of what I speak, but at least
I will not see it happen or hear
How others judged my failure
To comfort, inspire or to lead—
Take my bones to your breast
That I may at least contribute
My salts to you—

Observing

Light Trilogy: I. Mountain Light
He stands by the window outlined faintly
by starlight; on the other side of the glass
a thousand bright stars hang over
the mountains. Only from his small center
are mountains more lasting than the stars.
He does not move; behind him in
a small mirror starlight is doubled around
his shadow. A small universe opens
behind his eyes and he fills it with stars.
There are things about light that we cannot
measure—joy at connecting, a pine needle
on a layered forest floor. The stars over
the mountain change subtly.

II. The Age of Light
Light excites the empty field with its speed
and pushes time away. Light is not straight—
It follows the curve of mass, bent by media like glass.
It is absorbed and slowed; it is pulled out of parallel
and tangles with itself over shadows, creating patterns
in matter. Light may be transformed to flesh
and keep its energy low, or be released again
and flee once more to space where it grows heavy
with age and reddens, until nothing is left
but entropy's memory of heat.

III. Metaphysics of Light
There is light, but it is not seen.
Space is spread with light that pushes its field
in all directions but leaves space empty.
Trails of light are invisible from the sides. Points
in motion only are seen directly

as they enter the eyes.
Colors explode in points. The points
are meaningless. New ones explode
and push away old, which enter as orders
seen from the perspective of time.
We are paralyzed by the present
for all the richness we feel
and reach desperately forward
or backward, for simple distance.
We live in a metaphysics of light
and only need to look to our cathedrals
to be reminded. We have created a forest
of filtered mists where radiance is stained
and dimmed to fit our minds.
When the sun sets behind the sea,
its last ray is green.

The Ecstasy of Weeds

Diverse and fertile, weeds wait
Outside a profusion of possibility.
Lupine lies frozen for ten thousand years;
Thistles rest on fencerows and roadsides;
Chamomile waits to colonize vacant lots.
Our skill at gathering wild plants
   And herbs has been lost,
And with it the value of weeds—
Who knows that couchgrass heals?
We know nothing of them. Seeking
Leads into wildness: Bluebells,
Simple roses, spiral racemes.
Where shall my soul dwell?
           In immortal tansy.
And where is my home?
On earth in morning glory.

The Ecstasy of Trees

Some things cannot be measured— joy
when light and water strengthen trees
and they stand.
                They stand outside
of the plane of ephemeral life,
outside their own dead
flesh, outside the insubstantiality
of light.

Cloud

Once human, now dispersed
above the earth, particles suspended
together in constant motion—
tenuous, insubstantial, deceptive
but from your distance I look solid
and whole. Then slight temperature
and pressure changes let me precipitate
down, gathering lamina. As I drop
through layers, impurities
condense, growing

I fall
enter into bodies, cool machines, collect
in streams and pools, know them well
and depart, evaporate with the wind. Rise
out of touch and move again in shapes
of fantasy. Although I am bound
to the surface of the earth
by gravity, and though I must touch
you to live, It is the rising
and falling
I love.

House of Rain

When I was young, I built a house of cards
To live in, since I might want to move
quickly or change the gaming table.
I built it on rock (music) so it seemed stable.
One day a wolf wind blew it in. Aahhh.

I learned a lesson, and when I was ready
I built a house of wood, from pieces
Of an old sawmill, but I built on sand—
That was my metaphor for her—
And when she collapsed, it all fell apart
Although part of the gable sheltered me
For a while, until I could recover the pieces
I needed to live a while longer.

Now I have a house of rain
roof and walls, and floor of water
Diverted by trees and taken up by soil
And I am never separated from anything
From the sun or air, or night mists
In my house of rain, but it offers
Little protection, nor has it limits
That must be respected, but it is a share
Of the forest, so I never fear the pain
Of permanence or loss.

I will never live in a house of stone
Nor one made of tin or the bones
Of mammoths or dinosaurs.
I could build a city in the clouds
And I think I will try. The canvas
beckons and I have many images
to fill it, and if they do not last,
I can laugh, move on, remembering
My still beckoning manse of rain.

Driver

Her form was not perfect, but she drove it
towards its possibilities with eagerness. Her brain
was not large and convoluted, but she really
pushed it faster than others, worked it harder.
Only when she relaxed and talked recipes
And coupons did the West Virginia
Drawl and mispronounced words make
Her seem uncomplicated or slow.
She focused on something and worked out
every detail, then worried them into a beautiful order.
When she became successful, and identified a partner—
me—she focused on him and pushed and pulled
and shared a new trajectory. He was smart
and stupid in his own way. I suppose that's true.
They developed together in ways most others
did not, driving and reaching, then slowing to
consider the connections with others, and
the consequences, before expanding a web
making a place with extended family and friends
who shared some of their interests, and who offered
different perspectives and experiences. Sometimes
just talking or traveling. Sometimes sharing silence.
Everything she touched was changed, often improved
Sometimes made worse on occasion. Everything
she felt was expressed, sometimes accepted, linked.
The place where she lived was customized, for
Better or not. The things she dreamed made clouds
sometimes light, or dark, and influenced others.
She was generous and helping. What else is
accomplishment but this? She was thoughtful
and careful. What else is genius than this?
She flowed with air and water. What else is true
beauty but that? She is. Here. Living.
What else is there that matters at all?

Finger Play (In STEM: SpaceTimeEnergyMass
  & stanzas on pattern, emotion, abstraction, field)

Space. I watched your fingers
Play with the napkin and silver.
I heard your toes
Playing inside your shoes

Your soft words played
With mine as we talked
To push the time along—
Bad idea, since

Time prefers to be drawn
And observed, treated
To slow heartbeats
Under a blanket of invisibility.

Later, I felt your hand
Play with my hair
And I saw the light
Play in your eyes.

Energy. My hand brushed your leg
And confounded the space
That we occupied together
With what space preferred.

I saw the glowing halo
Extend itself into my
Own surrounding field
As they both merged.

Mass. A tingling feeling
Awoke a response
As my cells converted
Chemical shapes to energy.

As we moved closer
The fields became denser
I watched the curve
Of molecules as they swerved

Towards a new pattern
And contributed
To its size which changed
The shape detectably.

Then we were carried
By the whole configuration
You and me and all
Our baggage and such.

Emotion. Our beloved bacteria
And strange components
linked us closer to the other
breathing dimples in the field.

Because we thought we knew
What we were, we invested
The pattern with a name
And prescribed its boundaries.

We abstracted the essence
Of what we understood
But then dreams and desires
Warped the pattern of that field

With what we wanted and needed,
And as the years passed
And the pattern kept developing,
It became too complex

To understand or explain.
We lived it until the field started
To fail and fall apart
And by then we knew it was mortal

But it didn't matter
Since we had lived it fully—
Then the frame shifted
To a different universe.

Dancing Between Shadows (For MER 1966)

I saw you dancing by yourself
in a room half-dark with memory,
felt gravity loose its gentle bonds
and the earth slow down while you spun
wordlessly alone, almost unseen,
twirling around in a dream
flying away, you know, with me.
What music have you always carried so,
how many thousand miles ago?
Where would I look to find
the origin of that celestial motion
that keeps the footprints on the rug
two steps behind? I saw you turn
with your arms folded on your bosom
but ready to sweep any unwary
preoccupied man, child or record album
into your exciting embrace.
I saw your legs move through your skirts
I saw your hair unbound and flowing
I saw the light in your face.
How many times was this the joy's
only possible expression,
how often lifted you from depression
how often was all direction lost—
the entire world left behind—
that you could discover the one within?
All the stars were spinning, and planets
and stones, falling leaves
were waltzing in a whirl
turning to snowflakes in a swirl
in clouds spiraling like atom-patterns
dancing around you, and you—

She is One—

She is all women I thought to myself
And so, incomparable.

Rest your head on her lap
as she lifts and fans your hair
and she is Delilah.

Have her tend some bleeding wound
with cotton at her fingertips
and she is Nightingale.

Argue about life with her,
taking sophistic pleasure in thinking
and she is Hypatia extending thought.

Become lost in her wildness
losing your compass or guide
and she will rise as Diana, your protector.

Dismiss her with lies or misplaced desires
or notice her minimal flaws
and she is Lilith.

But, no I am foolish, she is not
all women or the worst or best
but a metaphor for womanhood

In one mortal body—bitch, whore
goddess and creator
Sweetness, mine.

Deep Kiss

I. I want a deep kiss
    I want a slow fall
Into the restless horizontal
    What you have I need it all
I need more than you can give
More than you ever had or will
    And I need it all
Until it can make me still.
I suggest you borrow against
your future or distill something
from your fruitless wringings
    unconscious stirrings
because I need it now.
    I need to fill myself
Because there are so many holes.
    Old friends gone
Lovers dead or moved on.
The universe has so many holes,
    Some filled by stars,
Others—I thought I could fill
    Myself but I was wrong.
There are so many more
outside and I watch the flow
Because everything flows and fascinates.
    But, I need you to try to fill me.

II. Kiss me one more time—it cannot be
enough. Kiss me now. I want to stay inside
until we're hot and dry and then—
                        kiss you again
and we will repeat everything in reverse
and all time's appointments will subtract
themselves from the universe until we're left
barefoot in the clouds—nothing else but that.

Simple Time Travel

Spent the evening traveling through time.
The past was very easy
Held by photographs and old records
But the future really tested
My imagination.

I saw you finally reaching your goal
To be an architectural engineer
And head a company of peers.
I saw the old Subaru we kept driving
Ten more years, I saw a few pieces
Of good furniture from yard sales.
And you with your 95%-reduced
Price dresses and clothes. Some new
Electronic devices for productivity.

Then I extrapolated a few trends
And anticipated the stresses
And fears that wore us down.
But, then life continued in the bodies
Of our heirs and I watched them work
To offset the decline of civilization
And the disruption of nature.

In short, I finally understood
what people have always had
to do to survive: Choose and make
a better world through actions
and when it is time, let go.

The Future Unfolds with Us Inside

What a wonderful, wild time together
The future

I had come to the mountains to expose myself
to danger, to test myself and die—or to survive.

Then, I met you, and it all started with just
'One more kiss and then I'll go' or maybe it was
'one more question: What do you want to know?'
That was on the porch in Dupnitsa.

I wasn't ready to share any or everything
but it seemed so right to start it then.
I still wanted adventure and tests, but
Now I thought you might want to share them.
Everything would be new and different.
A perfect idea in hindsight.

We got married in a secular ceremony,
In a marvelously large, empty state hall
with modernist metal sculptures, and pledged
our children to communism.

We moved to a small village in the mountains
And worked for a national park, first surveying wolves,
Then trying to coordinate a society of craftsmen
Who worked leather, wood, bone, wool,
And sometimes paint on canvas.

We followed wolves from the park around the mountains,
In blizzards, windstorms, sunny days, and cool evenings,
Taking photos of tracks and picking up scat, identifying
Their size and sex, puzzling over their paths and lives,
Ignoring our own for a time.

Back in Richmond, unemployed for a while,
We found jobs teaching and shelving books in a library,
Then in a clinic. No government jobs as promised
So, we invented two novel niches for money.
Now, the adventure is different, still unpredictable
In the short run. We don't know what will happen,
Probably just get slightly slower as we age …

In my dream that night I say 'I love you'
But, did I say it waking? I cannot remember
And I ask, 'do you?' Love me, I mean?
Why should either of us ask by now?

Moon Light Lake

Under the moonlight whispering through
The glass of soft reflection, we talk
About unromantic things, mortgages
And bills. Such unimportance.

A glance at the lake outside
Then back to the tabled trivia.
Now we will always be under
Moonlight Lake—Never to escape
Never to see or reflect.
Unless we can rise to the surface.

I see the light cross your face as we stroll
on the old boardwalk. The day steals away
as though it could never stay too long.

I see the light dance across the water
as we canoe into the dusk then get
bitten by mosquitoes as we race
swatting and laughing to the cabin.

The wooden bed is hard, even with the sleeping
mat and bag. I lay down and gesture to you,
but you stand looking—I know what you see.

You see the light across my grave
as I imagine your face for the last time
and you walk away quietly—but you knew
that I could never stay
as long as we both wanted.

I am floating over Moonlight
And you can always visit me there.

Dreaming

Wild Apples

Aphrodite's Fruit
I picked the first apple
And received the name of the spirit:
Melus, melon-bellied Melus
Old priest of Aphrodite—remember?
The spirit of the tree reborn
In blossoms, consummated in fruit.
I polished it and held it up—
Reflections of a crow passing—
We broke it in half.

We picked the seeds from its core
Named them all each other
And threw them to the wind.
We floated down in slow embrace
Beneath a spreading tree
With branches reaching over
Us like arms in benediction.
Below us it sent roots to trace
The heart of water.

There is a time of critical need,
There is a distance where bodies react
And a reaching toward critical mass
When all the rules change
And qualities become strange.
Boundaries decay with energy's
Conversion, saving, and release.

Cocoon of Light
Caresses caused phosphorescent mists
To rise above our heads.
The sun spun sheets of light
To cover our delicate flesh.
The light became thicker
And dropped as we quickened
And made a cocoon with its threads.

We suffered the weight of moments
As if all time had stopped
And the past collected and pushed
Until all space had burst—
Sweet, golden, amniotic net
All twisted bindings come undone
Then tighter round again
Sticky, silky, shining skin.

Oh, that we clawed weakly
Not wanting out too soon.
Muscles tensed, stretched,
Jumped, and then collapsed.
The hands became heavy and slow
The hands became heavy and held;
The eyes became heavy and closed.

Dream of Dionysius
In the morning three apples were picked
From the tree of knowledge
And brought to him for his meal.
He turned one in his hand,
The two sides of the apple
Were faces of the moon
One invisible, one visible,
The secret of life and death.

She carried three apples as gifts
From the tree of life.
He understood their meaning
And ate—
         fruit dropped from a tree,
Leaves turned and fell, as did he—
The body was burnt on a pyre
Whose flames returned to the sun.

I lay on my back, looking up
Through nine radiating branches
At the dappled sun.
I gazed on your face
As smooth as the moon of day
And on your white-limbed body.
I loosened your hair and put
An apple in the hollow of your hand;
The other held the absence of poppies.

From Umbriel Observed
The crust of light lay shattered;
The sun cracked in the sky.
We lay touching in grasses
Our hands clasped at our sides.
We were as we were before, unless—

We have been tempered by our burning.
Emotions have their gravity
Attracting more around them.
We are a focus of particles
From everywhere. The energy
Of motion concentrates in us
Until we cannot hold it in—
                              Explode
And rise beyond the clouds and out.

The orchard is a galaxy of trees
Then it is gone. There is nothing
But clouds and whirls of blue and brown,
Vapor trails from the earth and moon.
We rush outward on a wave of light
Passing the wrecks of asteroids.
The stars coruscate like blossoms
In a field of black. Looking backwards
From the limit of light we see
The dwindling bright circle
Like a polished apple whose red heat
Hides the white interior.

Bad Dream Coyote (for MRR 1978)

Driving on highway 95 into Idaho, I see an injured
coyote by the roadside. I stop, get out, and lift him
in the back of the station wagon, an ungainly Buick
Road Bastard, next to my brother Mark's body,
in the back, wrapped in canvas. As I am driving,
I try to read from the Tibetan Book of the Dead—
only a pencil of light hits the book braced against
the steering wheel—to raise Mark from the dead.
His body had been interred for thirteen years and
much had been eaten or rotted away—but I do!

Raise him! Then he collapses. Shifts immediately
into the body of the coyote. The fresh coyote is confused
and agitated. He keeps jumping over the seat to look
at me. Then jumping to the back and defecating. I try
to explain to him that it's an accident—maybe the best
that we could do. He sits in the front, tentatively licks
my hand. I stroke his head. It smells of shit and wet fur
in the car. I open the passenger window a little.
We drive down the road without headlights. His nose
rests on the glass edge of the passenger window,
taking in the clouds and streams of messages from trees
and animals. I think he is happy for the chance
to breathe again, but he has a hungry look now
and I have nothing to offer but my arm—
or my heart …

Eve in Dreams

The highway is a snake, over the hills
between rises, next to the river,
through a wild forest then a cultivated
field of wheat, between houses and cities
and it offers one the fruit of knowledge
At least the knowledge of movement
faint connections and sometimes one's self.
What is the fruit? The city? An apple?
Who are the takers? Pioneers? Planters?

The river is a snake in a morphine dream:
    A snake drinking water
While floating on the river. It flows down
me but not inside me, but the outside is
    the in, no matter how I follow.
—the monster of energy destroys
everything. It is the mask you remember
as it devours you. It is not the beast, no,
but the teeth that you feel
as you are ripped into pieces.

Great love may arise from great tragedy
But yours predated that, Eve.
It was primogenetic
Love without name
Or terror.

Lilith from the City

We hear your voice moan over Ur,
Harrapan, Fatihpu and Tikal,
Daughter of night.
Created simultaneously
An opposite made, but undominated,
The ideal of the dream.
Too equal for Adam,
You flew from his stubbornness
To an unjust punishment.

Come from your ruined cities,
Consciousness of night,
Show us your benevolent side—
We have learned to trust our instincts
And will not be confounded by reason.

Release us from the single vision
Of civilization. Shatter the wall
And reconcile us with Nature,
Oh, mind of the wild.
Return the idols to the soil,
Be midwife for our rebirth
And help us return to the sensual earth.

Throw your power on the side of the low
Until wholeness is restored, open
The gates of empathy, let it mingle
With creativity. We open our hearts
To your spirit, Lilith.

Piñata of Dreams

I could not reach the piñata of dreams
as it floated just above my head
a transparent blur, a whale floating in
the ocean of air, cello-wrapped boxes
transparent each with a line
waiting to be touched and drawn
through the ribs in the side.

I reached my arms straight up
from my bed rolling on a mattress of air
and shuddered as the whale breached
in the sea suddenly near my grasp.
Anxious now, I drew the bluish form
towards me

A bubble, like dreams that pop
at my touch. And so it did, lost forever,
except a fuzzy memory of presents
out of reach of a stick.

Ecology of Fire

Fear fire, for it can move out of its place
Fire goes where it wants   it goes where
It can   it moves too fast   it wastes
The savings of light in leaves
Then, it turns on itself

Fear water   it can break you seeking its place
Fear wind   for it has no place
Fear earth   because it is your place
Fear all the choices you have to make.

Floating Clearly

I was aboard a dirigible, I know.
I was looking at the passengers
As we passed quietly through
The mountains with snowy peaks.
Suddenly, I saw through the masks
On every face—the man next to me
Had the real face of a brown dog
With a wet black nose, but
He was still dignified in his mien.

A woman stood by the window
She was a jellyfish with a delicate
White carapace over spindly tendrils;
I could see her lunch being digested.

Something was backwards I realized
It was not masks that made us different
That all loving beings were valuable
And equal, but the masks made us
Human because we feared our real self.

As well as less, more, or interfaced.
Some of us took masks and wore them.
Others made their own to seem
More complex, noble or stronger
Than they actually were.

I was surprised that there were not
More eagles and dolphins, but I knew
The excitement of being a monkey or rat,
Bacterium, cockroach, squirrel or whale.
I wondered if I could be all those beings
In time, with enough life and energy
And patience or luck to persist.

The blimp dissolved, we all were falling,
Except one who was a gnat and another
Who was a tern. I myself was a bear
So I prayed I would land among salmon
In the stream, but it was not to be.

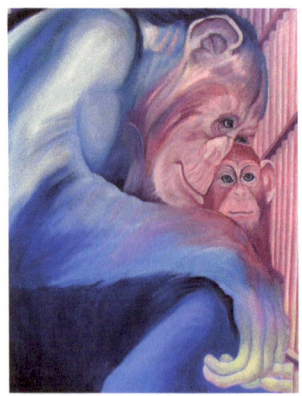

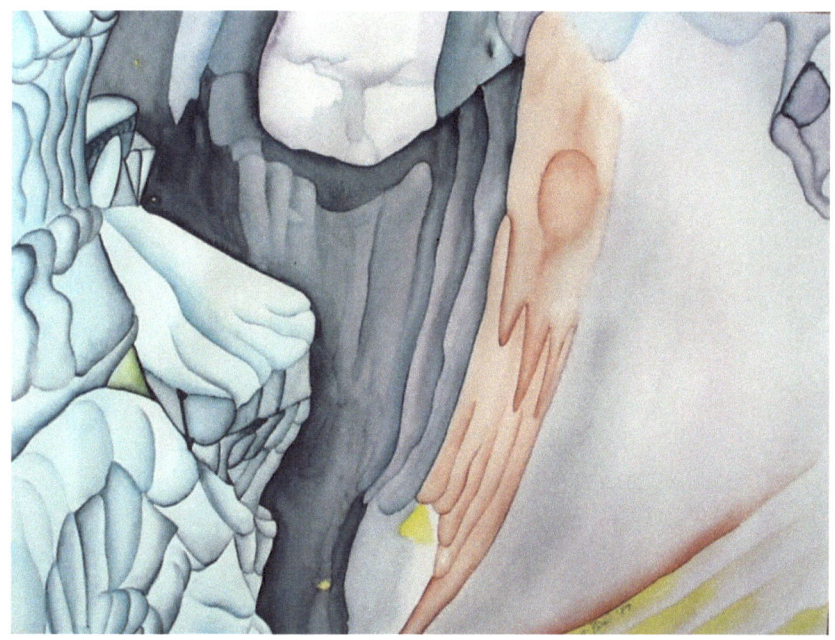

Heart of Beauty

Can anything be really equal? Must
Everything in the universe be unequal?
Not just things, but feelings
Abilities, friends, wealth, and beauty?
Is that the worst sentence we are under,
knowing everything is always different?

At the heart of the universe is beauty
At the heart of beauty is the universe
At the beauty of the universe is heart
At the beauty of heart is the universe
At the universe of heart is beauty
At the universe of beauty is heart
Beating, rolling, hot fleshy heart
And still, cool, hollow beauty
Powering and pushing the infinite
Unnamable, unrehearsed, universe.

The Reach of Water

Is the blood in we humans
Related to the sap of trees?
Trees are standing water, and see farther.
Does water circulate between them
exchanging ideas?
Does it remember the sea?
Is water the sea extended into dry air
or space?

Is the ichor of insects
Related to the fluid of molds?
Do they circulate?
Can the sea crawl and fly now?

How far is the reach of water?
Is all water connected in a global pool
like the atmosphere?
Perhaps that is the function of tears
to be borne upward by air.

Contained in travelers in space,
will the sea escape this planet
And reach for another?

Is it the act of reaching that matters?
Does the sea of a chlorine planet
reach also beyond itself?

The Ground

These leaves have fallen before
With a falling that is older
Than we who watch.
And this limitless falling
We see with a vision older
Than the falling itself.
When I touch you
The coincidence of having
Touched you those countless times
With the freshness of touching you now
Dehisces my body
Into two overlapping leaves
One eternally repeating what
The other finds new for the first time
One speaking what little can be said
The other feeling what cannot
One touching the other touching
Both intertwining in spirals
About you, my ground.
To see is to see farther than the trees
Whose leaves have fallen into space before
Toward a ground that is older
Than our vision.

Leaves

One leaf, then another, frees its stem
And weaves a spiral down—
The leaf we see in turning becomes invisible
And another appears. This is the operation
Of mystery: Leaves turn and present us
With the strangeness of a hidden side.
They tease us—from a different
Perspective, the leaf we think we know
Turns and disappears; the new side visible
We see and name and it becomes invisible
Again. Leaves only acquire full existence
By turning.

Turning is revelation: secrets
Open. Things turn and are renewed.
The earth rotates and revolves around the sun;
The sun rotates and revolves around the galactic
Core; the galaxy rotates and revolves around
An empty center.
Which way do wolves turn, before lying
down? Which way do whirlpools turn
Or whirlwinds? The twist of oak or sycamore;
The maze of tree and lichen, or rock and moss;
The twist of a hole dug by a skunk; snakes
Coiling; the lay of cedar or balsam fronds;
Hawks wheeling, shrikes hunting; the turn
Of a shell; the helix of light or the spin
Of galaxies?

Wolf Trilogy

I. Wolf Loves to Hide (For MWF 1994)

Weeks went by as I watched fruitlessly
From my night blind on the hill
overlooking the dusty trail.
I realized later that wolves love to hide.

All Nature loves to hide
And nature loves to play
Play at hiding, hide at playing, display,
show and turn and expect you to remember.
We remember, sometimes, even as we see
something again and the present expands.

Nature loves to hide and tease
But wolves love to seek.
Humans love to seek and please
And so we seek each other and play
And hide within nature, our places,
their places, all the natures that exist.

II. Wolf Story

I am wolf. I chase the deer who chase the grass
who chase the sun. Grass is light, deer is light, wolf
is light—all is light. Across asia, siberia, america, europe,
I chase deer and mice and light. Not alone, no, always
with a family, always at home.
                        I was raised by my parents,
uncles, aunts, brothers, sisters, and friends. I learned
cycles of heat, the meanings of clouds, the scent of prey,
the feel of grass—the culture of our ways: how to play,
and hunt and play. I found a mate, we played, shared

mice and moon and fluid—our way of mating is beyond
you—we lock and turn and we hold and hold until
we are dry and fall apart. We made a den; cubs came
from us and we joyed in their presence, teaching them
how to play, how to find food and eat, play and sleep
and eat and play.
                We were many, a populous people,
until your kind came with sharper teeth, faster claws,
greater numbers—many, many more—and took
our homes, our places, our food. There were fewer
places, fewer pups, fewer of us, then almost none—
and light has lost so many of its facets.
                              I am wolf.
I am old and stiff. I need to piss—
Ah howl with me one more time for the missing
and the unborn, for lost worlds and lost light—
now, howl!
      (chorus)

III. Wolf News

This is what I, wolf, see: Tracks, lines, bent
stalks, small prints in dirt—but there
are primary trails: Vapors, clouds of smell,
the history of all who passed before me, their mood
and direction, health and intent, messages
that cannot go unread, only evaporate
and be replaced by newer ones, layer
upon layer of deep rich sediment, exhalations,
urinations, oils, saliva, hairs, and excretions—
the signs that let me taste who ranks, who rejects,
who mates, or not, who travels, who kills,
who sickens, who is at home, who is not,
whatever is dropped, brushed, torn, left behind,
whatever can be carried by wind and air

and can tell me the story of the hour, whatever
I can use to complete my own needs
and understanding, though there are things
I do not know—how does a butterfly die? Does it
just land, fold its wings and wait, not to fly again?
Does time slow, or being extend?
My own death may not be as easy,
but you can smell and taste that story later.

Shadow Play

Wolf folds
        shadows
around her shape to move unseen—
    but the shadows remain
a few moments longer
after she is gone, for me to see.
The air adjusts slowly to her absence.

A shadow plays
with her source   with the observer;
       the forest hides
the shadow, but the air above the grass
    anticipates her form—
and lets me reach her, almost.

Changing Lightly with the Mountains
(Промяна Леко в планините)

Things fall away from us like leaves useless
to trees in winter. We keep what we need,
and rather than use dead memories for defense,
we let them decay to prepare the soil
for our annual regeneration.

You worried that your past was an unwanted
burden on the delicate threads that connect us,
but experience should not weigh us down
like unwanted baggage—it should contribute
to our transparency so that our thoughts,
our motives, are perfectly clear,
and eventually we will not be seen at all
standing in front of the mountains.

Memories

Mountain Bluebird Echo

I recognized the bluebird call like an echo
from across the valley. An echo, but nothing else
is needed. Another call—and echo turns back
to us changed by cliffs and water—ecology
is nothing more than hearing and tracing
the connections through the gaps of nature,
the gaps that support our freedom.
The echo resonates with the past and others.
Everything returns if you can absorb it.
The bluebird is an echo of the color of the sky
the color of water and sky combined in flight
made flesh in a mountain bluebird, insistent.
He brought spring and took summer light.
Before he goes, I beg him, Fric, fly back to me
for an hour. Fly back and properly say goodbye
with dives, hovers, and rests, and sitting
on my shoulder. Fly back, so I can listen to you
one more time, hear your chirping song.

I cannot wait a year for your return. It's too long.
I will be underground by then. Then I realize
that it will be no different than the year your valorous
brother Frac did not return to the fence post
on the trail—I've seen some of your tribe leave
in the fall and not return the following spring—
That is how life is filtered—just by not
returning when expected. So please glide back
and sit on my wrist and chirr so I can breathe your colors
in one more time then dance in the air myself once more
and rest. Fly to me as I breathe your name and if you
have died to hawk or age let my power resurrect you
so we may both rise to some heroic altitude and fall back
slowly in one last flight together.

The Wasp

I watched a wasp drift down to the forest floor
And sit on a leaf without moving—
Hours latter topple to his side and curl up,
The wings reflecting the light
And catching tiny currents of air.
How long can a wasp continue to fly
Without a need, without a reason?

How long can a heart continue to bear
The sadness of indisputable collapse?
How long can a ghost continue to haunt
A place without a receptive fit?
How long can a place continue to thrive
Without a flow of difference?
How long can difference survive
Without change or regeneration?

What is lost? What is generated?
What is the pattern that permits
The continuity and vitality of flight?
What is vitality but the rapture of energy
In a very limited renewing form?
What is death but the collapse of the pattern
And the release of the captured?

It is all within limits—too much energy
Overwhelms the form, too little
Lets it drift gradually apart.
What is the universe but a chance
For everything to exist in a form
For the wasp to exist with wings
To appreciate its self and its Self
To be as large as the very universe?
Like you or like me?

My Heart Breaks

I watch you get dressed in the closet,
Buttoning your blouse neatly
And my heart aches

I hear you telling Geveya she cannot
Go to school dressed like that
And my heart breaks

I remember you leaning over me
As I lay in the hospital bed
And my heart breaks

I recall the week we hiked
Through the mountains
And down to the lake

The water was too cold
But we splashed around anyway
And had to take

To the sleeping bag
To get warm again
But sat up to stay awake.

I run my finger on your cheek
and trace your lip
and my heart breaks

I remember the last time
I ever touched you
And my heart breaks

It breaks for the last time
From the sheer weight
Of happiness!

Forgetting You

Sometimes when you look at me
I can see everything that you see.
Sometimes when you listen to
The sea, I can hear every rise and fall.

Because we're close, because we feel
The same, because we are the same
In many ways, that harmony can cause
Just as much pain as joy.

So, we have to be apart enough
Different enough
For a little disharmony
And we have to be separate
Enough and different
Enough for difference
To have meaning

So I offer you this: That I will forget
You from time to time,
Ignore you in the morning
And afternoon of life

So that by dusk
We can be closer together
And the rhythm will join
Our hearts and minds
In a curious syncopation.
What do you think?

Like Beasts (For MRR 2003)

Every year, around the equinox that measures
the length of light and the depth
of my loss, a thought slowly opens in me
that you died on this day.
So every year I stop and think
knowing that you cannot—I remember
where you are and where I am
that day and this year I was in a mountain
wilderness lying on yellow grasses
watching clouds reform like fantasies
in air, feeling the mist fall on my face
and wondering how much higher
I could climb before the light faded
and determined where I had to rest,
and I think to you: You could be with me,
if you had not thought that an hour's loss
was more important than lying together,
brothers just the two of us, like beasts
beneath the sun and rain on a bed
of mosses and grasses—having collected
all the intervening days of listening
to other voices with other messages, other
attractions, distractions, and dreams,
and then conversing about them.

No one misses you like your brother
but I am only that and I was not there
to countermand your decision to die
the one that should have been mine
and I only wait now, and you wait I know,
but I no longer hurry, for time is not mine
any longer; in the depth and chaos of the flow
I am only an eddy, collecting experiences
for us both, a few thoughts and a few words
that I cannot rehearse with anyone else.

Tain's Gift

I walked into my forest—
Mine from the same conscious vanity
That let me name animals and trees I had come
to know, my pines, my deer, my salmon, my hawks.

The walk from town—along the highway
Then the road to the trail then the deer path—
Had been exhausting. When I reached the stream
I fell gratefully to the bank and sipped some water.
I had planned to deny myself that but it did not matter
I was here. I was almost home.

I rolled over, feeling the mosses cradle my back.
I looked up through the pattern of branches radiating
From each tree and crossing to cover the shrubs
and grasses between the trees. The light radiating
from the sun was filtered until only a few rays
reached a lucky patch, mound or sapling.

I watched the clouds block off the rays one after
another as they moved across the sky. The clouds
had risen from the breathing of the trees, from
the rhythmic daily taking in and giving out.

I stood and walked uphill looking for Cherisbend,
a tree who marked the center of my territory.
As a youth an old white fir had fallen on her
almost pinning her to the ground, but she
had turned to grow straight again towards light.
When the old fir rotted and broke under her knee
there were two bends that made a decent chair
for an enterprising mammal—anyway, me.
This natural seat encouraged philosophy
or at least daydreaming. I continued walking
not having seen her yet.

I recognized an old beaver breather hole
and knew I was close—the stream had shifted
and the beaver dam had been abandoned.
The slope had been leveled by trapped dirt
and it made a good elk bed now and the leavings
of the elk made a lush spread of grass.
Snuffblow, the lead elk, lead his troupe here
to spend the night. I skirted the bed and hiked
up to the flattened shelf on the hill. I could see
Cherisbend now, a distinct shape next
to all her straight neighbors. I looked up to see if
there were buzzards gliding above the trees.
Four pines over, Highroost, a pine who had been hit
by lightning that killed the top, offered a flat
plate of large dead limbs as a landing site for birds
with large wingspans, buzzards or eagles.

At Cherisbend I dropped to my stomach
and looked for Sporethief the vole. The hole

looked like it was still used. I looked two trees
to the west at Owlhinge, a fir who hosted
a spotted owl, Bandido, with a taste for voles
in the net of life and death, of which I was part.
And, I had come here basically for one reason
And one only: To surrender my life and heart
As a gift to the forest who raised me,
Who found no fit in the city of lies and cuts.
I flipped on my back and rested my feet on the bole
of the tree. I watched the game of light and shade
a while as I wriggled my back between the roots
and stretched my legs over the ground.

I closed my eyes and slept. The breeze played
above the trees but it could not reach me. When
I opened my eyes it was dark. I heard a sound
and recognized coyote steps, probably Tandreen,
trying to get enough mice for dinner.
Dinner was something of my past, like ambition,
building, love, and finally breathing.
I was wet, never completely dry
I was cold and shivered on my back
my ears were shut my throat raw.
I saw angels in the tree, wings like green
boughs. It was quiet, time slowed
and I was finally still
and warm again.

I don't know how many times I slept, just
that it was one more than I waked
My vision closed until it was
a tiny spot of light
in darkness—
comforting darkness
like my deep forest soil.

October Afternoon (for CJH 1986)

I opened the curtains, brushing
brown Celtic patterns;
you lay down.

I lifted the window and turned
and stood still while you
closed your eyes.

The wind brushed your hair as you
were falling asleep.
I saw it stir.

The sun touched your cheek when
you rolled on your side.
I heard you sigh.

Wind and sun and memory held
you so you could not move.
I only wanted to—

Perception Like Candlelight

She washes her face by candlelight,
No neon stage or fluorescent store
Just a single candle by the mirror.

A face that age cannot identify
In the gentle glow, nor tension flaw
The halo blending into darkness.

We see each other so, with
Perception like candlelight.

A Pharaoh's Sleep (For ELW 2013)

In bed, under covers—in a very Egyptian position,
Perhaps like a mummy, maybe Pharaohs slept like
that when they were alive—I placed my hands
crossed on my chest. It was hard, cool, and unmoving.
I left them there, but things did not change. I wondered
if I was dead—
          Suddenly I remembered putting
my hands and then my head on my father's chest
just as he died. It was hard, cool, and unmoving.
I had turned away to look out the window when
His breathing had stopped. Perhaps his soul flew
by to distract me. My brother's gasp made me
turn and race to him.

As I touched his chest, I suddenly remembered,
or thought I did, that after I was born I probably
touched his chest the same way, only then
it was firm and warm and moving from his heart.
I once asked him what I did when he held me.
He said I laughed; I was the happiest baby

That he had ever known. I even laughed
While I was dreaming.

I felt my hands still resting on my chest, shaped
Like his, cool and hard. I could not be dead,
yet, but it was a strange feeling. Maybe most
men's chests were like that just after death.
I knew women's were not.

My mother's was soft and cool, but then
I was holding her when she died. I suppose
I am lucky to have held so many of those
closest to me as they died. It was always
so quiet, less crowded, but afterward,
even though I captured her last breath
I was less.

Now I weep over memories as much as I laugh.
I know Marishimira will be upset when she touches
my chest after I die, but I knew she will accept
this part of the living cycle. She has
no choice of course.

There are memories so strong they warp the steel
of our resolve, so hot that they melt the frozen
mass of reason. That is stupid. The heat
and strength are passed on to beating hearts
and pulsing minds. The memories of the dead
are unreachable.

My chest was still cool, so I put a sweatshirt on
Lay back down and placed my arms over
My chest and tried to go back to sleep. I wanted
to dream of flying and falling wildly out
of control into the warm Nile.
All that would be left is my voice.

A Lady's Dance Card (For MER 2013)

Good-time Charles did not
Get his name on the card.

She stood along the wall, pressed
against the collapsed bleachers
Waiting for Evan to get there
And ask her to dance.

She looked at the small wooden card
For the Forestry department dance
Lionel Hampton had already started.
She glanced at the gym ceiling
So high above, draped in ribbons

She felt a tap on her shoulder
And turned—it was him, untying
His tie, explaining why he was late.
She smoothed his black hair
And left her hand on his shoulder,
"Let's start, now," she urged,
seeing her blue in his black eyes.
"It's half over. Wait, let me catch
my breath. Shall I sign your card?"
"If you want," she said, commanding.

The history of their romance
Was recovered in forty dance cards
That were still in her father's cigar box
After they had died, he by accident
she shortly after from a broken heart.

Druidess of the Tuatha de Danann

She lay propped up by pillows
Having dispensed the last words
Of advice to her listeners.
She closed her eyes, so
No one saw the force of light
That was filtered by the blue.
Her hands were clasped on her chest
White on the white gown.
She looked a Druid priestess,
Elder of the Tuatha de Danann,
A mass of white curls dangling
In a fringe around her head,
As bald as all Druid elders were
Women and men, old or young.

We asked her questions, one by one
But she only sighed as lightly
As the breeze through the window.
We interpreted what she thought
As what we wanted and sought.
I stood beside her, the successor
Elder and gently smoothed
And lifted her hair. I could
Have answered since it was my time,
I could have tried but I knew
My voice was raw and weak.
She held the oak piece in her hand
Letting it list to the side.

Finally, I read some lines from a book
That had no meaning beyond sound.
Perhaps the minds that received
Them would make them more.
Two short breaths and her chest
Stopped moving. I bent to hear

And captured her last breath
To carry to my lungs to be exhaled
again for the others to share.

We all touched her lips one by one
Then gathered in a broken circle.
She was a motionless Druidess
Preparing to enter the oak at death.

I keep the piece of oak on my desk
So that she is always near
And her words counsel my decisions.

Picture Wall

It started out as a painted wall in
The hallway. Then, a few frames
Were hung and it started:
Every unnamed cousin as a baby
Every aunt and uncle who might have
Sent a dollar and card for a birthday
Every grandparent and every parent
Cousin, brother, sister—
But not friends or places much
Not pets or captured animals
Not gardens or personal trophies
Not the people or places that shaped us
Oddly enough.

For those, there are drawers and closets full
Of albums, frames and loose photographs
Sometimes labeled sometimes sorted.
Maybe a few trays of slides or boxes
On the floor. Maybe a few in old wallets
Or purses in the closet. Their faces
Smiling with happiness pride surprise or
Understanding that they would be
Survivors on paper much longer than
In memory or life. In common with every
One the names are now forgotten when
Not attached to some clueless child.

Perhaps some anthropologist
Can put them in a catalogue like
Stars, digitized, in a database
For reference more than reverence
But at least collected and useful
In a way, not dusty, ripped, faded
Or lost to a landfill by confused
Heirs. Our inheritance is a race

Beyond the genetic—if only
The experience, the wisdom
Could have been saved
Or have been used to shape
Our wobbly civilization
or our treatment of the wild—
but it wasn't—and now we
have to grope our way to
health and balance
without the help of those
captured in photographs
mostly unnamed unremembered
who might have appreciated
the chance to show what they could do …

Imagining

Amaryllis Falling

I saw you under moonlight and you
Reflected me. I saw you under starlight
And you grew distant and mysterious:
Your skin was the color of evening
As if you breathed that color in
And pumped the blood of sky through
Your flesh—your nipples were darker
Than your breasts—your hair a deeper
Blue—your eyes held aurora lights.

I saw you again in the forest by day
Standing under the cedars
Swaying before me in green—
Your body was a tender shoot
Nourished by the blood of leaves.
Your limbs were lighter than
Your body, as if newly grown
And your face about to bloom.

I held out my arms to you
But you turned and ran
And changed as you did:
Clay and dirt made you red and brown
Rock on the cliff turned you grey;
You looked back once as you fell
Through air—

Bastet Holding

Bastet—bewitcher, bewilderer,
Savior from evil spirits
And mistress of all who travel,
Goddess of the Nile,
I knew you by your style,
Your flavor of decadence
The knowing glance of permanence
When eons were brief to your smile.

Queen of all unanswered questions,
Much reposed in you
That will never be spoken or heard
And all your ambiguities are obeyed
As mystic prophecies.

How old are you, how old is water?
Was there water when you first awakened?
How many times has your timeless
Body been refined by
The river of forgetfulness?

When you were born
Was the moon aloft to call the tides
And release them to the shore?
Is it you who measures seasons
And intertwines them with her colors?

Who is it who carries clouds
In the blue of her eyes
Whose eyes are like planets
That turn and bear storms,
Who holds the green of papyrus
By her side and welcomes sunlight home?

Heraklitus' Vision

The earth turns; sun lights forests
and fields, and they breathe;
matter feels.

Pines transform light to honey.
When the earth turns from the sun
the forest exhales.

Leaves disappear in flames
invisibly, radiating heat at night.
The forest is a burning house—
whole mountains burn coldly,
more slowly than stars.

Life is fire, and it does
not need a body of its own;
it dies and is reborn in everything.

We live by the interior touch of flame,
tenuous flame, dissolving weight;
is not fire the flesh in bloom?

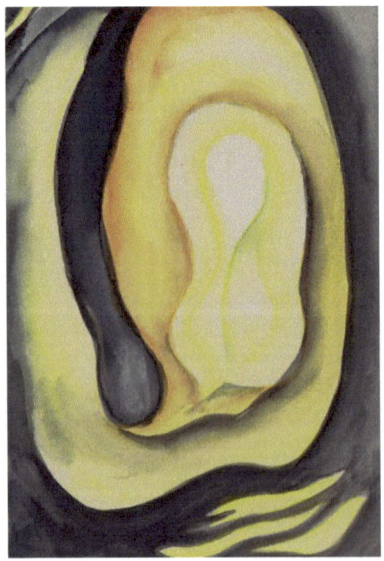

Aekus Humbled

"You had perfect wings
silken, new, ten-ribbed, white—
we tore them off—
on the cinder path
under cavernous air.
You cried out but could not move
in the absence of wings.

You had perfect eyes,
blue—no gold, and piercing—
they could make us move
or burn ours out—
we tore them out
and left you under the bridge
by the river of oblivion."

"Mother, father, crippled judges,
can you take away my perfect heart?"

Bear Masks

Bear masks, elk masks traced
On the wall of the cave.
We put on their skins and faces
To learn how they behaved.
They were kin and we needed them
As they needed wolves and men.
We took only the weakest,
The sick and old. Their strength
Was ours, and we would not let
It ever diminish or grow cold.

Now the elk are silent, photographs
Show only hide and not the motive.

The real face is never seen. Now men
Kill the strongest for trophies
And dismiss our art. The image
Of the elk is seen on metal cans
Cast away in the stream—The image
of the bear on boot polish.

We saw strangeness and sanctity there
Not the human stink on every feature.
The bear was our father, elk helped
Us to be human. We changed
Ourselves to fit the earth. We fit
Ourselves to please the earth.
You will share our fate—faster
Now in ignorance' full light.

The Cave of Night

She lay on her side, indifferent in sleep
Slowly music, and light
Dancers around a fire. One held up
a metal disk

She woke, gazing at the wall its smoothness
dissolved as from acid on
a copper Sesterce—Vespacian's profile
She blinked redimensioned.

The smoothness was scored with scratches
As she watched
Scratches outlined figures sharply
Across a fissure
Altamira, the code of mystery
Renewed in red.
The deer are running.

Alone in a World of Wounds (for JBC 1984)

We murder in ignorance or by accident,
A thousand ways in a thousand moments—
Every footprint leaving waste behind.

We kill for food or for convenience—
All living creatures feed on living;
Every hunger writes an autobiography
Of death. Our reverence is only
Acknowledgment of its necessity
And the fear of its consequences for us.

Our consciousness leads us from the whole;
That is how we know—in parts;
And that is its penalty. We must learn
Respect for iron, weeds, and flies
And grasp our way back.

Our obligation is to allow everything
That can, to exist, not to control, promote
Or extinguish, but let each thing reach
Its full development.

Our duty is to feel, not transform or save,
To live, not evolve or finish, to respect
That the whole may feel in its diversity.

Our destiny is to turn the wheels
Of mortality and be turned under
Ourselves, that the earth may turn.

Convolutions (Whale Stories)

How the levels of salt and water have changed;
   Which streams lead to winter plankton;
      What canyons too deep, what volcanoes to avoid;
       Where the floating shadows came to destroy;
And where the temperatures rise and food is scarce;
   Where cascading rivulets excite flippers
     And tumble the body until the cold
       Awakens the need to surface.

Songs, songs for saving thoughts of wiser,
   Farther-traveled individuals or tasting
      Great adventures—history of thought in sound—
       Beauty of speaking them again. Songs
For entertaining, for mating—giving
  Of sperm and air, for expressing the intricacy
     Of balance, for creating fluid ideas
       That crest and evaporate in spume.

The invention of stories to explain the working
  Of waves and the purpose of breathing,
    Indeterminacy of water, the strangeness of air
And its relation to death, the substance
      Of other intelligent beings—the role
    Of reason to mold the universe and increase it.

Forest Passage

I don't tell anyone where I am, just
like I didn't tell anyone there where
I was going. Now, I'm in the forest, but
I'm not alone, no, everyone here has heard
me stumble through the brush and vines,
but they let me go my own way. The painted
turtle could not escape and had to be held,
as unwilling as you but easier to catch.
He showed me the direction to the stream.
The bull snake path pulled my gaze to
the berries that were old but very sweet.
I poked into the old dry leaves that crinkled
with his passage—never did see him.

Fir trees protect me from the sun;
a breeze winds around me exhausted
from forcing its way past the edge

trees' low boughs, but welcome and scented.
A chipmunk scrambles out of reach
along a log, certain that I'm hungry
for her—and only her flesh.
Across the sky, the eidolons flirt
before turning into merely clouds
that whirl into other shapes.
Birds sing and let me know when
someone's coming so I can hide as well.
Turkey buzzards patrol the whole
forest just above the treetops.

I'm not upset, I'm not afraid, the harm
that's possible is not the cruel kind.
Bear rambles along, leaving berry-rich
piles of dung; I poke it with a stick
to see if it's still warm. It is.
Now it's dark, I walk through the trees
just slightly darker than the deer
trail slightly darker than the sky beyond.
A mountain lion watches without giving
away her position—I know because I smell
her musk slightly stronger than old leaves.

Every passing moment something human
slips away from me like night fog.
I am incapable of feeling, although
I can move quietly like a mountain lion
through the needle-dry trees.
I am as cool as the moss that grows
over old logs. I am as dark
as the soil under decayed wood.
I am as content as the black bear with
the richness of fall berries. Every day I close
myself a little more to useless information.
Soon I will be incapable of speech.

Heartless (Once a General Ache)

I heard a pretty song
And committed it
To my stolen heart.

But, I could not repeat it
Unless I filled the hole
Where that heart used to be.

I felt along the forest floor
And found a tender mushroom
And it agreed to fit
And become my heart.

So the songs I sing now
Connect me through filaments
To every tree and shrub,
Worm and vole, owl and trout.

This heart does not miss
You at all—it is
Much too full with the flow
Of sugars and sap.

It never aches for a disconnected
Disinterested body
No matter how divine
The form once appeared.

It never misses the strain
Of misunderstanding. There
Can be none, as complex chemicals
And simple charges never lie.

If you require the flash
Of electric excitement

Then the slow chemistry
Of being will never interest you
As it captivates me at last
And ties me to living.

Reflections On Surfaces (For LGS 1988)

I saw your face in the window of a 56 ford,
looking forlornly at the signs that passed
and I ached to comfort you and tell you
that your sadness too would pass
but I turned too slowly and you were gone
with the flow of Boston traffic.

Years later, on a sidewalk in New York
we passed suddenly and I saw that you
were resigned to whatever fate
you thought held you, and I wanted to tell
you that we could make a better ending,
but, again, I paused to wait.

Later, a decade later, on Micah lake
as the boat was speeding by the shore
I saw you sitting on the dock looking
at the water send its messages in waves
to you and I ached to hold you until
you looked at me that way.

And over all these years I waited wanted
and ached for someone I never knew
and so was unable to know those already
near to me and I suppose I will die pining
for what can never be, but I long to see you
one more time and stop you and say—
please stay with me at last.

Practicing

Moments

You always meant to smile
You knew it and you kept it secret
The joy that came through others
You saved and hid away
Until you were all alone
That moment no one saw
That no one even knew existed
That moment you saved
For a time to be renewed.

And, someday, when you're old
And all the colors turned with age
You'll remember all the moments
And think that's all that ever was—
The moments all were you.

Aurum Nostrum
*Aurum nostrum non est aurum vulgi.**

Little fires reaching through my arms
Reaching down my spine
You have fires too, as slow and
Eloquent as mine
And they move together separately
And will meet in time
Then time will disengage
And they will rage
And—oh—the joy of being consumed
Of having struggled so
And finally, fully, wildly bloomed!

*(Our gold is not common gold)

The Origin of Myth (De Origine Fabula)

Our bodies bend light, our love is like an egg—
Primordial cosmic ylem bound impenetrably in
One-way porcelain—
                        letting myriad senses enter
But nothing returns to the universe
From whence it came, untransformed.
Our bond is of a kind not nuclear or chemical.
The glass may be inspected from without,
Creatures may curiously peer in
Or sink infinitely slowly in if they get
Too close, but they cannot break in
And spread us out like spoiled fluid.
The egg could only rupture if a tide
Of feeling were to separate us—if the forces
Could not be balanced—
                            the egg would break
Our energy and pain would furnish substance
For those it intersected by its radiating
Sphere—our love become a myth.

Ille Terrarum

Ille terrarum mihi praeter omnis Angulus ridet. —Horace^

I cannot love you without the scrawk of jays
without the approval of coyotes we know by name,
without the rising and setting of the sun to align
without the ceremonies of corn and grapes
without the help of shadows and planes
and the hundreds of webs and lines and ways.

I cannot love you for long if the roots are gone.
Your sacred touch, untied, is not enough;
we are not strong enough, alone.

Failing Sleep
Nocturnis ego somniis iam captum teneo —Horace*

I lie awake and dream of you
I wake and dream of you
I dream of you

I dream and what I dream is past,
then I wake and what I see is past
and when I dream and wake then
I have you—briefly.

No position is complete
the goal of sleep:
To catch and hold you.

I try to dream again.

*in my dreams
sometimes I catch
and hold you

^That corner of the world
smiles for me more than
anywhere else.

The Place of Reconciliation (For VI 1973)

Sometimes I cannot wake you from your
        Larval sleep
When I need to tell you
    of a dream I had
        To wake to keep:
A rounded hill, overlooking the city,
    Grass still green,
We walk holding hands until we can
    No longer be seen
Then stylistically in slow motion drift
    To the ground
And hold each other tenderly, tightly
    Without a sound
Our history of troubles dissolved
        By the dew
Evaporated by the sun and carried by wind
    To a place
Where human concerns join with those of
    Other beings
Where feathers, furs, scales, or hair have no
    Special meanings.
Filled with that feeling, we walk back—
    I forgave your betrayal
And I never thought of you again,
    dreamed or saw your face.

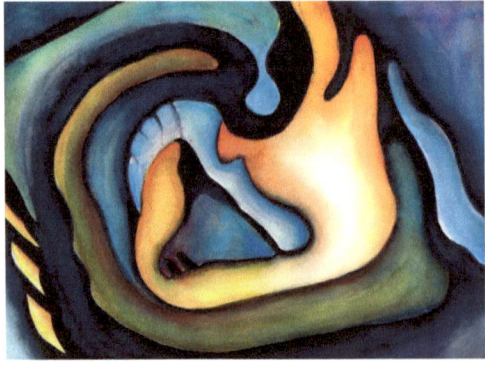

Leaving Palouse

Driving west at sunrise
on highway twenty-six across the Palouse hills
As I go down every hill
the sun sets in the east and as I go up every hill
it rises again, blinding
me in the rearview mirror.
I lose track of time because it seems
like I have been traveling for days. The days all look
the same, and I know that they are—
these are the very same days that I traveled
ten, twenty, thirty years ago.

A different memory greets me on each
curving slope: A flat tire
there, a picnic here, the day I raced

a Jaguar to the city
limits—the Subaru made the corners
better—you only screamed once as we took
the tracks in front of a train,
the night I missed a corner and ended up
in a ditch poised for takeoff
looking at the stars wink their light-years-late
hellos and knowing you were sitting
waiting with two glasses of wine,
green beans and potatoes on the table.

August brown bunchgrasses wave good-bye
and my tires hiss
their reply.
Shadows lead the way, dark fingers pointing
from dark pools. A redtail
hawk watches from a fence post satisfied
that things are right.
Only a sun-dried sagebrush
blocks my way and it is not enough
to deflect the momentum of a hundred
bad decisions and wrong turns.

If I thought I could turn back
time with each ascent and backward-setting sun
I would drive until the hills
were eroded by wear
and every one but me had given up
but the car keeps moving smoothly
and the illusion of progress fools
the tired, emptying
mind

—The eternal return does not require death after all—

Vous êtes mauvais pour moi (for HMM 1989)

Why You're Bad for Me
If I have crumbs on my chest
and you brush them off,
then I tend to be sloppy just
So you'll have to touch
Me. If my hair is mussed,
If my shirt untucked
Then I'm lost—
Being out of order around you is hopeless.

Why You're Really Bad for Me
I'm always out of breath
Around you. I can't control my heart
Or mind. I get a fever—you're no relief.
I might just want you to be worse.

Warning Signs
Fallen eyelash, accidental touches
Fallen hands, touching; tides; fallen
Bodies, deliberately touching.

Dangerous Conditions
Matter and antimatter.
Steam in a boiler. Dust in a silo.
You and me.

Dangerous Signs
Overexposure.
Radiation, energy
Clothing—its absence.
Touching—not.

Freedom & Practice

Into the bonfire went his paintings
freed from the flaws of expression
and the limits of simple skills.
The flaws disappeared
never to be seen or remembered.
He watched them move to dreamtime
by degrees, by particles
the ideas now immortal, waiting only
another instance of form
in paint or pencil.

The errors of the artist drive the process
of fitting a species to a rapidly changing habitat
and too much detail clouds the image
as it shrinks to fit the tired mind.

To scatter fragments in a circle
only fragments are left
but they multiply the pleasure of beginnings
So many fragments so much pleasure
a whole universe of pebbles
with no center
invites more practice.
Practice is enlightenment.
Beginning again is joy.
And the forms sublimate away
redirecting energy to the periphery
as the course is bent back to the stones
of a disintegrating statue
to be reassembled another way
Or not.

Marishimira [in Bulgaria]

Blue Stars

That day that you wore the blue print dress,
I took the time to look deeply into your eyes—
from the dress to your eyes
I moved through an infinity of blue—
I would be foolish to compare your eyes
to a shallow lake
or to the thin extent of sky. I know better:
In the constellation of Orion, there are stars
that color of blue, and only magnitudes of distance
shield us from their furnaces of creation—
and only distance from you now saves me
from total annihilation.

Through Tearlight (Чрез светлина от сълзи)

I was happy with you in dreams but I was afraid
to speak them to you, realizing our love
had never been and could never be—
I kept my feelings from you, and wept
for the loss of possibility.
                          But, each tear,
painfully torn and exquisitely formed,
then seen through, revealed other
dreams with you, other lives, and now
my reason for weeping is to visit
those worlds inside—
                In each world a new life unfolds
and in each I find you waiting
and in each I weep and subdivide
until my lives infinitely recede
like rows of self-reflecting mirrors,
    yet I believe that what tears separate,
eventually they will unite.

Our Daughter Eyes (очите на дъщеря ни)

That night after we talked in the quiet space
of a crowded sidewalk in Dupnitsa Center
    I dreamed
that we became lovers, seamlessly, completely,
then after a while married, lived together,
had a daughter Geveya, worked side by side
and aged under our tree,
                        then I died,
and you both mourned me quietly.

But, now, after work, after class, when I meet
you on the sidewalk, I have to smile,
because I see you have
                      our daughter's eyes.

In Wild Flight (В див полет)

The music was wild and never-ending—
your feet hardly touched the ground
before resuming their flight
turning you around without stopping,
threading your way through
the lumbering followers.

From a distant orbit I tried to match
your pattern, to match your joy
at moving and flow in a flight
of expression, without direction
without reason.

I stopped dancing—you continued.
I watched and in you I saw beauty
without awareness, laughter without pain.
Then, in myself, I saw love without desire,
love without words,
until now.

On Silk Pillows (For SE)
(На копринени възглавници)

In this decadent dream you invited me
with your eyes, shaded by those incredible
lashes, to lay down beside you
    on white silk pillows—

That moment is forever fixed in memory:
Your hair fanned out in a halo of dark curls,
    the fineness of your skin
made darker by contrast with the sheet,
the shine of moisture on your lips,
the lighter hair of your belle chose,
a small bruise on delicately curled toes
resting on cotton—
                  the threads
of small details tied us to that extended time
while I waited, before descending
to eclipse your glowing face.

And afterwards, we sat on concrete stairs
reading Bulgarian stories to each other
my leg crossed over yours, then yours over
mine and mine over yours—
                  a four-legged
animal just reading in a time crossed
with pillows and books, sheets and concrete
already anticipating the chance to meet
and explore again.

Snake Dance Flame Dance

Music filtered through turning leaves
and lights made columns of trees.
He rose and spiraled his hand, fingers
fanning down, and she nodded and rose
in perfect communication. Their paths converged.
They locked arms
                    and began to dance.
  An unsteady alliance at first
subject to the rise and fall of distant music,
      the hollows of one accepted
            the swells of the other.

The air seemed warmer the music louder,
the colors of their clothing contrasted and blended
      as they moved.
  Thought created patterns made by their feet,
as the feet moving forward drew
            those moving backward.

They held each other closely, whirled
then pushed apart and played arpeggios
in light.
        They pulled together and spun faster,
their steps not limited by the music
as the music changed to fit their steps.
    Once they became tangled and fell,
but the music paused for laughter
and it was apropos. At times the limbs
would intertwine in a hopeless tangle
          until one would rise like a snake
charmed from a basket and the rest
would disengage and flow away.
    Then they would break away
from the others and commence a chase
  across the floor.

The dance was a flame between them
    that flickered as they moved and blazed
again stronger as they touched.
   Light strung lines wherever they went
until the world was a shining web
    and at the center
               their dance.

Gathering Layers: Cut Geode

When we kissed the first time
It was with the shock of never having kissed before—
    oh, no, it was with the freshness of rain that,
having fallen, evaporated then precipitated to renew
itself, and that was the kiss, a renewal.

When we touched the first time
it was the unexpected otherness of a mirror image—
    no, no, it was like the surfacing
of a stone buried for geological time,
exposed again by movements so sublime—

Every kiss, every touch, should be so
yet gather layers that reveal the original each time,
like a geode. You have no past—
    no, you do, but it is what shaped
you and what with mine brought us together—

Let memory be stripped by dissipation,
The burden of experience be lifted by the lightness

of being, the vapor—
    no, rather let
the whole knotted
    fabric of life
simply unfold, and
    us within.

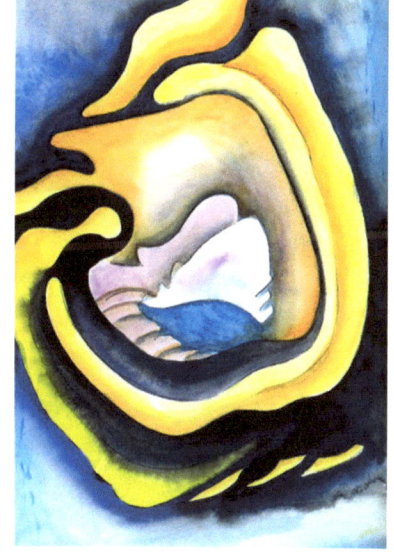

Propinquity (родство)

I saw you, read your formal bio
Then pretty much ignored you. Oh,
I was dragged to your birthday party
By a guy who thought you were interesting
And cute. I only went as a favor to him.

A week later, we walked together,
worked on a project teaching ecology,
Shared a Sunday afternoon.
Invited you and your friends
For ice cream floats just
So I could practice Bulgarian.

I asked you to dance once and liked it.
We danced almost every dance,
Then we talked all night, until it
Was too late for me to go home.
You undressed while I almost fell asleep.
It was a comedy of errors, the laughter
Almost spoiled what came after.

I promised to see you again
Some weekend if I could take the train
To the town where you were assigned.
After five weeks, I called you,
Then escorted you to a birthday party.
That was an intriguing shower
Before sleeping, after ignoring the others.

Weighed your assets, couldn't see a negative.
Decided we should share everything
Maybe combine our time and lives
And experience things together.
I was not sure that I loved you,
But I knew I would someday,

So I offered to marry you only if
We could have a two-year engagement.
It was almost another comedy of errors.

The minister wanted to marry us right away.
The American Ambassador agreed enthusiastically
(They were both in Russia when I was there
and were desperate to marry someone, anywhere).
The doctor checked our health for twenty Leva
And we arranged a day at the state wedding hall
Which was deserted except for the four lady clerks.
With our witnesses, a godfather and godmother,
We marched under the high ceilings past the glorious
Imposing sculptures of metal celebrating
The importance of the heroic people before us.
We agreed to the State's conditions: work hard, follow
orders, and pledge our children to communism.

In our Fifties, we did not plan to have children
Anyway. We honeymooned in my little village
And treated ourselves to French fries and coke
Which were more expensive than vodka and steak.
In the apartment, we listened to music just louder
Than the burble of the river below.
And I wondered—why I didn't think like this
thirty years ago. If I had met you then. Why didn't I?
And I wondered if you really loved me
And I wondered how things would be different
when you finally understood that I loved you.

Think. Great love can result in great disaster,
bad stars, as if your light was a kind of weakness—
But, it is great, isn't it? The body cannot love
only the mind, and its desire to fit inhibits
the working of the lungs or heart.
Let us rest a while, recharge. In nearness.

Every Thread Made Visible

In the new threads of the avocado seed
lining the vase I see everything
that is gentle in you made visible.
Under the vase on the marble plate,
I see everything strong
in you made visible.

Visible especially since my brain
is so tied to you that everything
is shaped by connection and strength—
Marble resists water and weight
but, the threads crack marble
the weight of time crushes threads
and the voice that speaks carries long
afterwards in lines and marble as faint
echoes in matter and memory.

Traces of Light

I woke before you and watched your face
at dawn—suddenly light flowed off
in waves as if it were alive
as if you had animated it.

I watched a moment, then looked up
and saw the pattern had been
reflected from the turning ceiling fan
and had been reflected off
the water outside the window
as the sun rose to light
a late summer day.

I lay back down on the pillow
facing you. I started to sleep
and dreamed that I could read
all the patterns of light.
I traced it through the trees and clouds,
the vacuum of space, back
to the sun, whose light
was just waste from transformations
into more complex atoms,
collected from the debris of expansion
the experience of being a universe.

I leaned on my elbow and looked again
as the last of the light from your face touched
mine and then the wall.
So ephemeral, but I knew it would repeat
tomorrow, if conditions allowed.
Where did it go?
Into the wall, a faint echo

In paint and plaster, into the mottled
brown fur of the cat, who slept
contentedly without opening her eyes
innocent of the play of light
or its echoes.

Too faint for me to read
but warmer, the memory
of your face and light
the tangled collisions
created a neural pattern
with its own interior rays.
Those patterns, from mornings
of reflections formed layer
over layer that informed the quickening
of our shared breath as you awoke.

One Little Drop
(Една малка капка)

When your heart stops and tears start
and they flow, and it hurts, or not,
and they cleanse the pain,
or not, I can't be there.

I can't hold you then
but you can hold me in your memory.
I can't see you then
but you can see me in your dreams
and, I'll move and laugh and hold you
and tell you every lie and truth you need to hear
and I can say that our time was too short
and the moments too joyful and dear
and nothing else really mattered
even if it did.

I wish I could sing these words some evening
But my voice would fail and shatter
So I'll just hold you another time
And you'll think the reason why
Is the same as it was in Aprilci.
—And, it is, in a way.

Keep living as wildly as you can
and leave me some flowers from time to time
and some molecule of me will drop
like some touch of honey to your lips
or be pulled into your lungs and I will feel
alive a little again, thanks to you,
always ...

Participating

Three Perspectives from an Ancient Irish Forest

June
I. I lay down in a grassy depression. The lines
I thought were roots were bones, as white
as eyes, framed by a thought that a spirit might
match with mine, might offer a wild
pulse to my heart and link another mind.

II. The bones rose up and held him lightly, as if
they were mere fingers of light. The form spoke
of its life as a wolf of the wood, how it lived and died,
how it lay down one last time on the pine needles
and let its life exhale. I heard the sigh, the words.

III. My spirit found a home, another hunter
as clever and loyal, another expression
of the impulse to breathe, to prowl,
to taste of life, the chance to howl
for every storm, and run and dance.

July

I. I was sitting under the alder, admiring the many
mushrooms—my hands reached into the soil
and brought up masses of threads, fungus roots,
the symbiotic net that holds the forest together,
orange, white, gold—I tasted a few. Tired, I lay
down on the spongy forest bed. When I awoke
I felt refreshed, more alert and complete.

II. She was here, we touched, then my filaments
blended with her flesh, probed her cortex cells,
and what she was missing and what I was missing
filled in. I enhanced her ability to draw elements
from the soil, air and water and she gave me new
elements, a wonderful new mobility, and a way
to speak to the moving others—the eaters.

III. The forester was sitting under the tree examining
something. She rubbed it, sniffed it, tasted it, smiled
and lay down—colored threads swelled over her
suddenly then receded back into the earth. I paused,
confused by what I had seen. Then she arose, turned
like someone blind, until her eyes focused on me,
golden orange highlights flashed in her irises.

September

I. In the Cork countryside, I walked outside the woods,
looking into the shadows for the source of movement.
I saw none but went in. I waited by an oak. Alone,
separate, waited longer, until the shadows covered me.

II. Someone courted us by walking around and pausing,
coming inside; but he went no further and we could
not move to him. We waited beside him and he waited
beside us, until the ground and shadows connected us.

III. I saw him walking, then go into the cove and as
he reached into the trees, his arms lengthened
and the roots came up and branches lowered until
I could not tell where trees began and he disappeared.

October

I. I saw her lying beneath an alder, in brown lace;
I went to her and lay down and touched her face.
Her brown hair hung over me and through its veil
I met her eyes and on my side I felt her fingernails.

II. He appeared, as I was lying with a beam of sun,
his handsome skin, like my fur, shining with health
and need. He lay beside me and offered his life
which I took in my need and made a part of mine.

III. I watched a man walk directly through the forest
to where a bear lay in the ambient light by her den.
He lay down directly and touched her muzzle; saliva
rolled from her mouth, running down his cheek
and disappearing, then, as she tore him open
with her claws and feasted on the sweet remains.

Horses Under Lightning (Cavallo Sotto Fulmine)

All afternoon warm humid air rose above the hill
overlooking Vidima. The horses were pastured
in the orchard in the portable electric
corral by the house.
I brushed insect eggs from the black hair
on Roma's chest. You doctored the cut
on Figurina's leg; we both had to push
Ballerina's nose from our work.
You said she had to be trained soon. She wickered
agreement and we laughed. The dark bay
looked just like her mother.

Then we talked on the porch as the sun set
to the sounds of horses grazing. Roma stood guard

against every shadow or unexplained motion.
The air was still unstable, waiting to be overturned.
Unseen in the forming cloud the collision
of moving particles redistributed charges.

We went to bed as the cloud built over us and slept
until violent booms woke us. The cloud had reached
maturity, smashing air, rattling the windows
with hard rain. The horses screamed.
With a dead flashlight and an empty lantern
we went outside to calm them. The rain soaked
us instantly, one gasp and it was already too late
to get back inside. The absolute dark forced us to stop
and wait less than three feet from the house.

We had to wait for each flash for a tenth
of a second of light before moving a step closer,
after which the darkness deepened even more.
I took Roma, you the mother and daughter.
I did not want to be here, but the barn
was half a mile away.
We had to keep them from running.
Roma was wild and rearing, each movement
a still picture illuminated by a stroke of light; I reached
her on the fourth try. I stroked her neck and withers
slowly with one hand keeping the other on her chest
to track her. I whispered soothingly into her nose—
a bolt showed white-starred face and frightened eyes.

It was like being on the floor of the factory
of creation where electric power—ten thousand amps,
a hundred million volts per bolt—surged between
the generators. Charges built between the negative cloud
and its positive shadow on the earth
until they exceeded the insulation of air.
The current flowed in a path to a proud cedar
   and the return stroke flared at the ruined vertex,
   then went out—

                    Left a perfect wooden cone—
     a small flame flickered
into the ground around the trunk, an instant
with the heat of the sun. The path and stroke hit
too fast to tell apart. A crack and instantly a bang
as air exploded. My teeth hurt my ears hurt.
I saw the sound bounce off every thing—I saw
the waves vibrate air and trunks of trees. I watched
the tall cedar—my favorite for sitting under—
smolder, suddenly destroyed.

Another strike destroyed the southwest corner
fence post, you said. I saw you now and then
made still by a flash. I felt myself absorbing
energy somehow or maybe just vibrating
in sympathy. The horses were wild. The night,
the light, was wild.

After an hour the lightning moved northeast,
rumbling as different parts of the cloud reported
their progress, or differences, with the ground,
or unhappiness with the attitude of another,
light flashing between them.

The air had turned and balance was restored.
All things recharged. The rain became steady.
The horses were calm and hung their heads
in the beat. We stood beside them, looking up.
I did not want to move.

We went back inside, left clothing soaked
on the porch. Every night since has been pallid
and dull, except sometimes when I look
in your eyes and see the ghosts of lightning.

Light Pieces

With vision we make order to banish chaos
But vision illuminates the chaos clearly.

The wild sky sings—
  The air and light—
Not imaginary colliding particles—
  And chaos lives!

Practicing this is enlightenment.
Making light is enlightenment.

There are things about light
  We cannot measure—joy
  When light pulls up grass
Things about being together
  We cannot name—
Running through the woods
At dawn, leaving a few clouds
Of breath and stirred leaves.
  Each word is a piece of memory
    A memory a piece of living
I live on

Swimming At Night in the Black Sea
(Плуване през нощта в Черно море)

Swimming slowly then looking back,
amazed at how far away the shore
has become—I think
that I have not demanded enough
from myself. Is there more
that I can become, by extension?
I know the land is under me beneath
the water. What could happen?

It is not water I fear but darkness
and if I pray often enough for light
then it will always be like being
on the inside of a pearl
or on the wave in front of a ray
of light between shadows
and it will not matter if I sink.
The light has been captured and will
accompany me to the deep.

The Center Can Never be Reached

Lying on the bunch grasses, feeling
The dirt beneath and some of the roots,
I thought I felt the rock under all,
    Weighing on layers over layers
Until the pressure of that shifting mass

Compresses the shape of brittle crystal
    Into smoothly rounded glass
Then into a molten iron core.
Molten stuff moving outward
Seeking openings pushing cracks

Cooling in softened dullness
Then swelling and splitting
    A rare perfect crystal
Breaking through continental plates
And mysteriously diffusing in dreams

Creating clouds of soot and heat
Broken by patterns of sharp colors
Sending glowing sparks up
    Like meteors before falling
soundlessly to earth, near me.

I have turned towards the source
Passing through a warning chorus
Of nuclear voices lost in the chaos.
I may be reduced to disorder myself
Before I have touched the center.
    But, I cannot keep from reaching—

Do Not Ask Me Why

I've learned a few things (not that many, though).
I know why the leaves fall in October and I know
why the gopher snake bites when you pick him up.
I know why water runs downhill and where it goes
and I know why an owl flies and the lichen grows.

The leaves fall because the maple protects herself
from the dark and cold, and a snake bites
because he doesn't know you or your intention.
Water seeks a resting place, a stable situation,
the owl has to catch her food, and lichens
are trying to split every barren rock open.

But don't ask me why you left me—did you need
to protect yourself? Did you not know me?
Did you need a place to rest where I would not pester
you? Were you hungry or did you just want to degrade
me? I don't know. I really don't know why.

But, I do know that now I am more at home
with snakes and owls, squirrels and lizards
than I ever will be with your ambitious neglect.
I know why a coyotes howls, but not why
I must learn to. I know why a lion hunts
and rests alone, but not why I continue to.

I don't know why some swans don't mate for life
while others do. I don't know why some wolves
never mate and others do. I know why I want you
for life, but I don't know what you want—
I don't know and I know you cannot tell me—
and I worry that it's too late, but I don't know why.

Is it Just a Smile?

When God made me he put essences of other beings
Into my body: Piece of wolf, bit of crow, a few needles
from a pine tree, a spot of fungus, some worm, chunks
of rock, a little beetle wing, whatever else was lying
around. Then, I enjoyed being with all my relatives
and I was at home wherever I was.

But then I loved you and you made me more human,
so much so that I neglected the older connections—
almost forgot the possibilities. We kept to the concrete
city and exclusively human things. We celebrated human
differences and human heights, but then you left me
for a simple human being—you told me to leave
and stay away.

So now I live with real people again: Owls, lizards,
grasses, coyotes, lichen—without you. I see them
and yet I have not forgotten you or the time
I was almost dead. I run quietly through the night,
ruthless, hunting. I lick the blood. I sit and fumble
through the soil. I lay, empty and full. I shred bark
and twigs, tasting the not-quite-sweet cambium.
I open under the sun, extending tendrils down between
roots, between diatoms and water drops. At last my
shredded spirit is diffuse; maybe it will never return,
but maybe it does not need to.

Now the city has crushed you and now you need me
and I have come to help you, but when I show my teeth,
are you sure it's just a smile? When I caress your head,
when I explore your fingers, is it because you
are my mate, or just my prey?

The Way of the Deer

There is a way of knowing
That is the way of the deer.
You will realize you know it
That you are already like
And unlike the deer
In feeling and thought.
The deer embodies experience;
The vitality and wisdom of
Her body ruins complete rationality
And loosens up our categories—
No monster Pan,
But a small being
Pleased at fitting between
The woods and fields so well.
How can you browse grass or rub
A tree without becoming it?
Dizzy with eating, exposed,
She scratches the surface
Of wholeness with her hooves,
With her green eyes.

In a Vanished Forest

At a magic convention in Ireland, I scoff at a woman
trying to teleport two people to different places along
a wall—it would be a neat trick. I scoff again louder.
She invites me to be one. So, I agree. She says, 'you must
say the words, Far Invaray, three times.' I ask 'three?'
She says 'a mathematician could.' I say 'I am only
an accountant who keeps numbers straight.' She says,
'Listen to me count to ten, subtract the two and count
again. Get to six and then eight but to be complete
in the witches table nine is one and ten is none.'
Then I count too, and I hold a leg iron on a pipe—
the pipe tingles but no one moves. I wonder
though, about the feeling. She blames me for being
skeptical, ruining it. We argue through the meeting
that first day. Black eyes. Her name is Cairrean.
That night I buy several small ice creams for dinner
at a newsstand. On way to the camp ground, I meet
Emer, Tuathla and others. We talk. My ice cream melts.
I sleep on a mound in the park, near gypsies, cold
on damp grass, by an apple tree, no blankets, no peace
from memory. The sharp tongued winds of the north
they thirst for my damp breath.

The next day more weak magic. Cairrean asks me
if I can do magic. I say 'yes, of sorts.' She says: 'for
example?' She and cohort of young nice-looking
witches, all slim with black hair, but different heights,
have been teasing me. I am attracted to Moira
but their teasing is mean and I do not answer,
only listen and observe.
That afternoon, we are all walking in the holly woods
outside Blarney Castle. After a while Cairrean speaks:
'Salamander coil and glow, sylph smile and disappear
Whoever is ignorant of the properties and powers
of the four elements can never master them.'

Nothing happens. So, I look around and find
some willow poles on the ground, someone cut a while
ago. I find a few nails, some blocks and make
a small set of stilts. One of the boys Conchobhar tries it.
I say 'that is magic!' I make a taller pair, which is used
by another girl, then figure I can make a really tall
pair that can only be reached by someone already on
stilts. That works too, although it is hard to stop
and get off. The witches seem peeved. They ask
for real magic. 'Now.'

Then a young deer walks out of the oaks onto the trail
near me. I stay still. The deer walks by me, stops
and touches my hand with her nose. I look at
the witches, then down at the deer's front hooves—
blue and green paisley swirls, as if just painted.
I point out the hooves to the witches. The deer looks
at them, leaps the fence and bounds back into
the trees. Flash of white.

We walk on. The witches ask me if I can call animals.
I say no, only thunder. They ask me if I will. I say no.

But I lower myself down. I crawl like a snake
to see the roots, looking at ants and filaments
of fungus—I stand suddenly. Cairrean says
'the lightning is near, the sound of a jay
the whir of a bat the newts are in the bracken
the tree roots move like serpents in the soil.
And everything coils and soon
we will fill the air.' I cannot answer. But I hold
my arms out from my side. A snowy owl lands
on the wire fence opposite me and sits with both
wings outspread. I look; she looks; everyone looks.
She drops off the fence on this side to the ground.
I think she may fly away. I put one arm to my side
and the other hand on my shoulder. The owl flies to
my shoulder. I move my hand to cover my head so she
will not strike it. She taps my fingernails with her beak.

I crouch down. The owl drops to the ground. I stroke
her head and back. The younger girls and boys
come closer. I ask them if they would like to touch
the owl. They say 'yes,' and several do tentatively.
I notice the owl's claws are painted yellow and red.
The owl flies back to my shoulder; she seems heavier
and larger. I ask her 'are you a gypsy?' She says,
'who?' I say 'I cannot begin to guess your name nor
would I dare assign you one.' She says 'then you cannot
know me.' She now has spangles; her legs are longer—
she more resembles a little girl dressed as an owl.
She has colorful cloth with silver threads around
her waist. We talk about magic, its weakness,
disappearance, pretense, and current hiding places.

Suddenly it is dawn. She is standing beside me about
four feet tall now. I ask her if she must go. She says
'it would be best.' I help her to my shoulders to fly
into the woods. She leaps outstretched but lands face
down in the grass—she is more girl than owl. I run
to her side and help her up. She blows air over

her feathers in exasperation. 'Too long,' she says. I kiss
her, but her lips are already hard. She is smaller.
I lift her and launch her again into the hazel trees.
As she glides away from me she seems smaller yet.
She lands on a low limb, glances back, her neck
twisting all the way around. She flies up to a larger
branch, perhaps confused by the light or just
uncomfortable. Then she glides by an alder tree
in the dark forest, becoming smaller until she is gone.
I look for feathers; there are none. I look at the sky;
it is overcast. Everyone has gone. No one ever
noticed my costly reconstructed forest—
vanished four thousand years ago.

Isle of Joy (L'île de Joy)

Inland a way from the ocean I was lying on grasses
with some fading flowers next to a pond. The sun
had just set and I could see the bands of darkness
pushing back against retreating light.
I turned towards the pond and looked at the still
Water with small complex waves
Probably from the wind or spin of the earth.
I watched and listened; the pond darkened too.

I looked at the patterns on water and decided,
rather than decipher them, to recreate them in my mind.
I turned on my back and looked at the night sky
and beyond, to the vacuum and dust between stars.
I could feel the basic waves from the first expansion
and the gravity of larger aggregations,
the long deep rhythm in my bones.

I could feel the pulsing molten core of the earth
and the wobble of its spinning laid on top
of all the other waves. And I could feel the drag
on the water as it sipped its boundaries

and on the air as it slipped between trees and leaves,
the harmony in my muscles.

Even my own breathing put its mark on the surface
of the pond—and I knew it remembered
all the waves that had passed over and through it.
And, I could see how patterns were made,
the melody on my lips.

I turned again and trailed my hand in the dark water.
There was a tentative touch and I focused on the frog
trying to test me as some strange rock or log.
I saw my dark reflection—it was Debussy's face.

I could feel so much then, the rustle of the jay
above and the keening of hawk as it missed its prey.
A dragonfly folded her wings. Slowly it all faded.

I realized that what was left was simply joy
and I did not have to know why.
I did not expect it again. The sky
became darker but I no longer worried
for myself or for my shining isle.

Verona ReBow Artwork Cover: Oceano Dunes (Oil on canvas 20x26)
Page 3. Double Delight (Oil on canvas 16x20)
Page 11. Waterfall (Watercolor 14x18 Framed)
Page 14. Coming Home (Oil on canvas 32x40)
Page 17. African Buddha (Oil on canvas 19x19)
Page 19. Composition No. 5 (Watercolor 9x14)
Page 22. Blue Oaks (Watercolor 16x20)
Page 23. J.S. Bach Works for Lute (Oil on canvas)
Page 28. Brahms Piano Concerto 1 (Oil on canvas 27x40)
Page 30. Birches in Autumn No. 1 (Oil on canvas 34x43)
Page 35. Beethoven Symphony No. 6 (Oil on canvas 28x28)
Page 37. Tree in Spring (Oil on canvas 28x36)
Page 40. Wind in Poppies No. 1 (Oil on canvas 36x48)
Page 42. Untitled (Oil on canvas)
Page 45. Vivaldi Concerto (Oil on canvas)
Page 46. Paradise Lost No. 3 (Oil on canvas 24x30)
Page 47. Sunset in the Canyon (Watercolor 11x14)
Page 48. Dunes No. 5 (Watercolor 16x20 Framed)
Page 53. Composition No. 6 (Watercolor 9x14)
Page 54. Dunes No. 1 (Watercolor 16x20 Framed)
Page 57. Cranes Flying (Mural)
Page 58. Chopin Prelude No. 15 (Oil on canvas)
Page 61. Autumn 09 (Oil on canvas 23x27)
Page 64. Birches in Autumn No. 2 (Oil on canvas 33x45)
Page 69. Oak in Spring 09 (Oil on canvas 17x21)
Page 71. My Mother and Brother (Watercolor)
Page 74. Composition No. 3 (9x14)
Page 78. Paradise Lost No. 4 (Oil on canvas 24x37)
Page 79. Birches in Autumn No. 3 (Oil on canvas)
Page 85. Beethoven Moonlight Sonata No. 2 (Oil on canvas)
Page 86. Composition No. 3 (Watercolor 9x14)
Page 87. Sunrise (Oil on canvas 28x31)
Page 91. Oceano (Oil on canvas 24x28).
Page 93. Crane No. 1 (Water color 10x14).
Page 96. Brahms Hungarian Dance (Oil on canvas)
Page 97. Composition No. 8 (Watercolor 9x14)
Page 100. Composition No. 4 (Watercolor)
Page 102. Morning (Oil on canvas 26x32)
Page 104. First Snow (Watercolor 16x20 Framed)
Page 105. Composition #7 (Watercolor)
Page 107. Oneness No. 2 (Oil on canvas 33x40)
Page 110. Poppyfield No. 1 (Oil on canvas 16x20)
Page 111. Pismo Beach (Watercolor 6x20 Framed)
Page 113. Opening of the Center No. 2 (Oil on canvas 32x48)
Page 114. Autumn (Oil on canvas 16x24).
Page 115. Self-Portrait 1987 (Oil on Canvas)
Page 118. Shamane (Watercolor)
Page 120. Birches (Watercolor 16x20)
Page 121. Poppies No. 3 (Oil on canvas)
Page 122. Dunes No. 4 (Watercolor 16x20 Framed)
Page 124. Dreams, Self-Portrait 1975 (Oil on canvas)
Page 124. After a Marathon 1976 (by AMC–Watercolor 24x24)
Page 125. Wind in Poppies No. 2 (Oil on canvas)

About the Author

Alain M. Caratheodory worked as an observer, then research associate in astrophysics for a number of installations, including the MIT Cambridge Research Laboratory, Lunar and Planetary Laboratory, and the University of Arizona's Steward Observatory. Finding that his experience followed Auden's prescription for poets, he has written in poetic, as well as scientific, forms. He has been published in numerous regional journals; since 1984, he has worked only on book-length themes. He confesses that he continues to work hard, keeping to the dictates of Wordsworth and Novalis, to be a good poet.

After the marathon
AMC water color 1976

About the Artist

Verona ReBow earned a degree in graphic design. At twenty-one, working as a graphic designer, she enrolled at the Academy of Art in Munich, Germany, from which she earned a degree in fine arts. About her art, she says: "I grew up surrounded by the romantic and mystic air of a river valley, with deep forests and green pastures. The comfort provided by nature opened doors to my imagination. These early experiences of the fullness of life wove the magic carpet, which has ever since helped me travel between different worlds. The essence of these inner journeys found form when I learned to paint, and ever since, painting has been my ally and career. The inherent beauty of objects and the profound potential of existence move me to create and communicate with and through the colors and lines, where the worlds of abstraction and realism are one."

Self-Portrait 1975

Colophon

The furious charge at the end
Produced on an Imac running
Text, Photoshop, Indesign, Acrobat
From hand-written notebooks
Outside Tallevast Florida.
Typeface: Adobe Caslon 11/15
Display face: Gill Sans 14/15

[*Fragment* 1975]
Our love is like a flower
Reaching toward light
Whose purpose is being
And joy at being seen,
Whose flesh is summer
And whose very colors
Are the earth in bloom.

www.ingramcontent.com/pod-product-compliance
Lightning Source LLC
Chambersburg PA
CBHW042307150426

43197CB00005B/101